DRUM STANDARDS

T0048765

Music Transcriptions by:
  Joe Labarbera
  Billy Boy
  It's Only a Paper Moon
  Seven Steps to Heaven
  The Surrey with the Fringe on Top

  Steve Fidyk
  Delilah Dances
  Fly Me to the Moon
  If I Should Lose You
  Take Five

  Steve Korn
  Israel
  Softly As in a Morning Sunrise

Text by Rick Mattingly

ISBN 978-0-7935-9663-8

HAL•LEONARD®
CORPORATION
7777 W. BLUEMOUND RD. P.O. BOX 13819 MILWAUKEE, WI 53213

Visit Hal Leonard Online at
www.halleonard.com

FOREWORD

"When I was a kid, I would buy every record I could find with Max Roach on it, and then I would play exactly what he played on the record — solos and everything. I also did that with drummers like Art Blakey, Philly Joe Jones, Roy Haynes and all the drummers I admired. People try to get into drums today, and after a year they're working on their own style. You must first spend a long time doing everything that the great drummers do. Not only do you learn how to play something, but you also learn why it was played."
—Tony Williams, from *The Drummer's Time*

The late Tony Williams would likely approve of *Drum Standards*, which includes transcriptions of some of the greatest jazz drummers in history: Art Blakey, Roy Haynes, Elvin Jones, Philly Joe Jones, Joe Morello, Paul Motian, Max Roach, and Williams himself. In addition to their solos and drum breaks from several jazz classics, the book includes transcriptions of their playing on the "heads" of the tunes, giving insight into these drummers' mastery of song form and structure.

To truly get the most from these transcriptions, however, it is important to hear the actual recordings in order to fully appreciate the nuances of touch, timbre and swing that contributed to the unique sound and style that each of the players represented in this book achieved. Information about the album on which each performance appears is included with the text preceding each transcription. So listen to the music, study the transcription, and then get behind the drums and learn from the masters, just as Tony Williams did.

DRUMSET NOTATION KEY

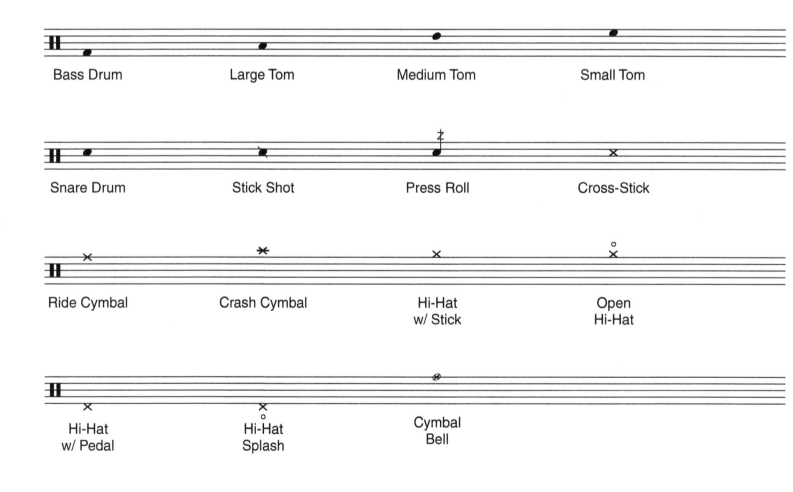

DRUM STANDARDS

CONTENTS

"BILLY BOY"
Album: *Milestones*
Artist: Miles Davis
Drummer: Philly Joe Jones
Label: Columbia

Philly Joe Jones said that his greatest experience in the music business was the time he spent with the Miles Davis Quintet, which included John Coltrane, Red Garland and Paul Chambers. "We were all learning from each other," Jones said in an interview from the book *The Drummer's Time*. "Miles was really the teacher. Everything he would say to you was valuable. Now, when I look back, I realize how much I learned from him about rhythm and time, and how to play around with the time and still have it right. That was a total experience."

In 1958 the Davis group recorded one of the most popular jazz albums of all time, *Milestones*. The track "Billy Boy" is an especially good showcase for Jones' talent. In particular, the "head" of the tune displays Philly Joe's mastery of brushes (and of fast tempos!). Jones was considered one of the finest brush players in jazz history, and this performance stands as one of the best examples of his finesse.

Also, in the following transcription note how Jones maintains a solid time feel during the "head" while catching key rhythmic accents in the melody. He obviously knew exactly what was going on in the tune.

"If I'm playing a tune, I really like to know it," Jones said. "When I'm going to play someone else's music, I try to sit down at the piano and play through it. Then it is easy for me to play it on the drums because I know what the music is about and I see exactly what it's doing. I don't like to take a shot at playing a tune I don't know. I never do that with my group. I tell everybody in the group, 'If you don't know the tune, *don't play*.' You can't play *at* it. If somebody asks you if you know a tune and you say, 'I *think* I know it,' don't play. Play it if you *know* you know it. I think it's a cardinal sin to play somebody's music wrong. Somebody sat down and wrote it out and worked with it, and then you play it and mess it up! Imagine how the writer must feel. So I like to play a planned arrangement. I know how we're going to start, how we're going to end, and I know how I'm going to color the arrangement."

But that's not to say that Jones planned everything he was going to play ahead of time. Once the musicians started improvising, Philly Joe was a spontaneous player who contributed to the excitement of the moment by taking chances.

"When the solos start, you never know what's going to happen," Jones said. "With my control of the instrument, I'll try anything. If I dream up something while I'm playing, I'll attempt it, because if I mess up, I know how to get out of it. I'll keep trying it until I do it. A lot of things I play are right off the top of my head. Many times, as soon as a thought comes into my mind, it goes right to my hands. If I fluff it somehow, you never know it, but I'll know it. There are a few things I won't attempt on the stand because if I miss it, I won't be able to clean it up. So I work with it in the house until I get it under control, and then I'll start doing it on the stand. I'll do it every night until I really get it down. Attempting things is dangerous if you don't have some experience."

The four-bar drum breaks in "Billy Boy," which were played with sticks, are classic Philly Joe. Although he was a definitive bebop drummer, his style was rooted in swing and his solos and fills always propelled the music forward. Philly Joe's licks were seldom difficult from a technical standpoint, but there was always a sense of spontaneity, a touch of humor, and a whole lot of hipness.

BILLY BOY

Traditional English Folk Song

Philly Joe Jones

6

B

Piano Improv.

A³

To Sticks

Four-Bar Breaks

Solo in B Section of Out Chorus
Brushes

Time

"DELILAH DANCES" (DELILAH)
Album: *Clifford Brown and Max Roach*
Artist: Clifford Brown and Max Roach Quintet
Drummer: Max Roach
Label: EmArcy/Polygram

Mixing Latin and straight-ahead jazz feels within the same tune was especially common during the bebop era, popularized by "A Night In Tunisia" by Dizzy Gillespie. "When we were on 52nd Street with Charlie Parker in the '40s, the Cubans used to sit in with us," Roach said in an interview from the book *The Drummer's Time*. "So we were intermingling and listening to each other."

But whereas most drummers would base the Latin sections of such tunes around a cymbal-bell pattern that imitated Afro-Cuban cowbell rhythms, Roach tended to rely primarily on tom-toms, as he did on the 1954 recording of "Delilah." (He used a similar approach two years later when the Clifford Brown/Max Roach group recorded "I'll Remember April.") "That had a lot to do with the Caribbean thing," Roach explained, "because I grew up in Brooklyn with people from Jamaica and Trinidad and places like that, so I heard that music all the time. And then when the Cubans came to New York, they would have four or five percussionists playing congas and timbales. I was really fascinated by that."

The linear pattern that Roach plays throughout the Latin section of "Delilah" reflects that influence, as well as his approach to the drumset, which he sometimes refers to as "the multiple-percussion instrument." But Roach never used more than a five-piece kit, and he recorded "Delilah" using only a four-piece drumset. "I don't need to have a lot of drums around me," Roach said. "A percussion ensemble has concert toms, the snare choir from piccolo to tenor, and the whole array of instruments. But the drumset itself is just that five-piece kit.

"The drumset is the freshest instrument in the world of percussion because the player has to use all four limbs. With all the other percussion instruments, we just use our hands. But the drumset uses all the technique that has been developed for playing drums with the hands, and having your feet in there adds other dimensions of technique. The variety on that set is amazing."

During the straight-ahead playing on the bridge of the tune, as well as during the other instruments' solos, Roach's bass drum is not audible except for occasional accents. But it's likely that Roach was maintaining a soft, steady quarter-note pulse, as he did during his solo drum breaks. "Drummers always played the bass drum, but the engineers would cover it up because it would cause distortion due to the technology at the time," Roach said. "There were never any mic's near our feet; they would have one mic' above the drumset, and that was all.

"It was funny to me that when I would hear a recording, I didn't hear the bass drum, because in those days the bass drum was always prevalent. You could not get a job unless the bandleader could hear that 4/4 on the bass drum. I remember standing in front of Chick Webb's drumset. His bass drum was so strong and constant I could hear it in my stomach: BOOM, BOOM, BOOM, BOOM constantly. Young drummers would stand there and say, 'Wow! Can you *feel* that?' Then, on 52nd Street, we learned how to play the bass drum softly. It was always there, underneath the bass fiddle.

"But you never heard it on the recordings," Roach said. "I've heard people say that, historically, I introduced the technique of *not* playing the bass drum and concentrating on the ride cymbal, which was not the case."

Nevertheless, Roach and Kenny Clarke are generally credited with developing the bebop drumming style, in which the ride cymbal became more important than the bass drum in maintaining the pulse, and in which the drums became more interactive through accents and syncopated counter-rhythms. Roach also moved into free jazz playing, and pioneered solo drum compositions such as "The Drum Also Waltzes." In 1970 he formed the percussion ensemble M'Boom, and he has recorded with a wide variety of artists, including classical string quartets.

"It's difficult to think there should be boundaries between genres of music," Roach said. "A lot of players have done things with Indian musicians, and I've toured with the Kodo drummers in Japan. You can always cross over and make it work."

DELILAH DANCES
(DELILAH)
from the Paramount Motion Picture SAMSON AND DELILAH

**Words and Music by
VICTOR YOUNG**

Max Roach

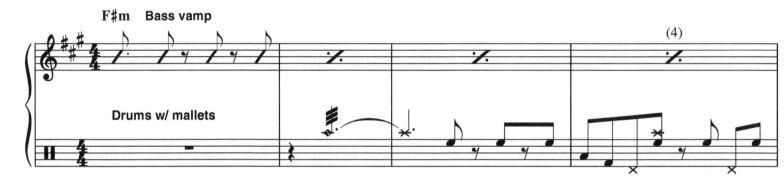

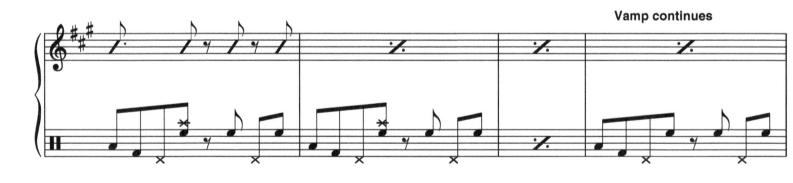

14

4-Bar drum breaks

w/ Sticks

Drum Solo
w/ Mallets

"FLY ME TO THE MOON"
Album: *Out of the Afternoon*
Artist: Roy Haynes
Drummer: Roy Haynes
Label: Impulse

"A lot of times over the years, when I wasn't getting too much credit for what I was doing, people would look at me like a new guy until they started checking me out and finding out what I had done," says Roy Haynes. "So for a long time, I felt like one of the best-kept secrets in jazz."

Born in Roxbury, Massachusetts in 1925, Haynes began playing professionally in Boston nightclubs when he was a teenager, working with such leaders as Sabby Lewis, Pete Brown, Frankie Newton and Felix Barbozza. After moving to New York in 1945, he spent two years working with the big band of Luis Russell. Haynes also subbed with Louis Armstrong's big band.

In 1947 Haynes landed a gig with saxophonist Lester Young, whose band often backed vocalist Billie Holliday. Haynes spent two years with Young, and then did a "Jazz at the Philharmonic" tour in 1949, after which he returned to New York and played with a number of prominent musicians on the famed 52nd Street, including Miles Davis, Bud Powell and Kai Winding, before joining Charlie "Bird" Parker's band, where he stayed for three years.

From 1953-58, Haynes worked with vocalist Sarah Vaughan. Afterwards he worked with Thelonious Monk, Eric Dolphy, Lennie Tristano, and Stan Getz. From 1961-65 he often subbed for Elvin Jones with John Coltrane's quartet — a gig that he found liberating. "I did what you had to do with people like Stan Getz or Sarah Vaughan," Haynes says. "But with John Coltrane, I was able to let it all hang out, so to speak. He understood what I was trying to do. Charlie Parker did, too."

During that time, Haynes also led his own groups. In 1962 he went into the studio with bassist Henry Grimes, pianist Tommy Flanagan and woodwind player Roland Kirk to record what is considered one of his finest albums, *Out of the Afternoon*. His unique style is displayed especially well on "Fly Me to the Moon," in which he aggressively punctuates the timekeeping on ride cymbal with syncopated accents on the snare drum during the "head" of the tune. And during the eight-, four- and two-bar drum breaks, Haynes combines military sounding rudimental patterns with over-the-barline phrasing, taking the listener on a series of rhythmic adventures but never losing the underlying pulse. The fact that Haynes drives a 3/4 tune with such momentum and conviction is a testament to his consummate sense of swing.

From 1965-67 Haynes worked with Stan Getz, whose band featured a young vibraphonist named Gary Burton. Haynes worked with Burton's influential group in the late 1960s, which included guitarist Larry Coryell and bassist Steve Swallow. Afterward, Haynes led his own band, the Hip Ensemble, which also played in the jazz-rock style. During this time, Haynes often augmented his drumset with timpani. "I got some five-star reviews with the Hip Ensemble," Haynes says. "We were a little different and there were a lot of things happening."

Haynes did a lot of recording in the 1970s with artists including Gary Burton, Stan Getz, Duke Jordan, Hank Jones, Art Pepper, Ted Curson and Joe Albany, and in 1979 he performed with Dizzy Gillespie. In 1981, Chick Corea, Miroslav Vitous and Haynes — who had recorded together in 1968 — worked together in Corea's Trio Music band, and Haynes continued to lead his own band and record with a variety of artists. He appeared on Pat Metheny's *Question and Answer* album in 1989, and Metheny appeared on Haynes' 1996 album *Te Vou!* In November 1998, Concord Records released Gary Burton's album, *Like Minds*, which featured Haynes, Chick Corea, Pat Metheny, and Dave Holland, and which subsequently won a Grammy award. "Roy was the only one who had worked with all of us," says Burton. "He shifted gears as he went from soloist to soloist and did what he knew each of us would be most comfortable with."

This "best kept secret in jazz" has been honored with numerous awards, including the prestigious French Chevalier des l'Ordres Artes et des Lettres in 1996. In September 1998, Haynes, Elvin Jones, Max Roach, and Louis Bellson were presented with American Drummers Achievement Awards by the Zildjian cymbal company, and that same year Haynes was elected to the Percussive Arts Society Hall of Fame.

◆◆◆◆◆

FLY ME TO THE MOON
(IN OTHER WORDS)
featured in the Motion Picture ONCE AROUND

Words and Music by
BART HOWARD

Roy Haynes

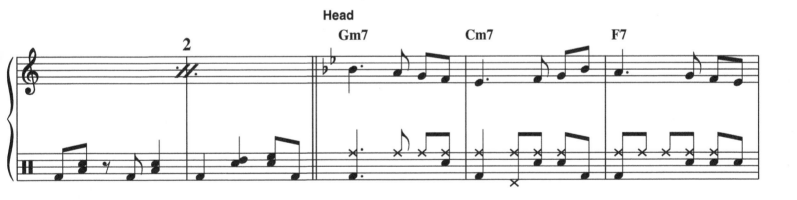

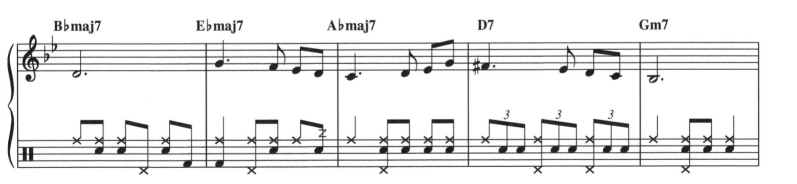

S.D. Press Roll

8-Bar Drum Breaks

4-Bar Drum Breaks

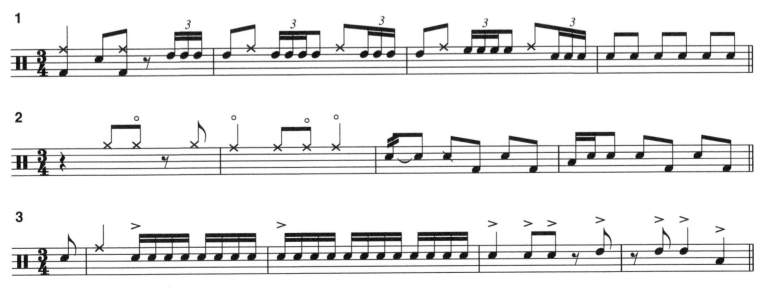

4

5

6

2-Bar drum breaks

1

2

3

4

"If I Should Lose You"
Album: *Out of the Afternoon*
Artist: Roy Haynes
Drummer: Roy Haynes
Label: Impulse

With solid roots in the swing style, Roy Haynes' early gigs established him as a master of bebop playing, and as his career progressed, Haynes was able to adapt his playing to a variety of styles including avant-garde jazz and fusion, without ever losing his own identity.

"My biggest influence was Jo Jones," Haynes says. "I also listened to Chick Webb a lot on records when I was a teenager, and then there were people like Shadow Wilson and Kenny Clarke, and of course Max Roach and Art Blakey. I tried to listen to everybody. I didn't try to do what everyone else had done, but I listened. My ears were always open."

The personal style that Haynes developed is characterized by crispness and finesse, as well as a tremendous sense of drive. His drumming has always sounded modern and very, very hip. Jack DeJohnette is one of many who credits Haynes as paving the way for the drumming of Elvin Jones and Tony Williams.

"Every time I read something about myself it usually says 'bebop'," Haynes says. "A review in *The Village Voice* called me 'hard bop.' I would have liked it more if they had said 'hard swing.' I'm not always comfortable with those labels that people use. I'm just an old-time drummer who tries to play with feeling."

Although Haynes' playing may be built on the "old-time" value of swing, he took a very modern approach to the subject, with the result that in a career that spans more than fifty years, Haynes has constantly been associated with musicians on the cutting edge. He worked with such artists as Lester Young and Charlie Parker in the 1940s, Bud Powell, Sarah Vaughan and Thelonious Monk in the '50s, Stan Getz and Gary Burton in the '60s, Chick Corea in the '70s and '80s, and Pat Metheny in the '80s and '90s.

A key element in Haynes' style is his ability to imply a sense of swing without confining himself to the standard swing ride-cymbal pattern, which is obvious in his playing during the "head" of "If I Should Lose You." Not only does he dispense with the traditional ride pattern, at times he omits the downbeats of the bar. And yet there is never any doubt as to where the "one" is.

"Charles Mingus used to tell me that I didn't always play the beat, I *suggested* the beat," Haynes said in a *Modern Drummer* interview. "You don't always have to play 'ding dinga ding,' but you've got to have that 'ding dinga ding' within yourself."

Haynes built his extended solo in "If I Should Lose You" on a series of two-bar phrases, played in answer to downbeats supplied on every other bar by the piano and bass. The overall impression is of sticks dancing over the drums.

"A lot of people describe my drumming as 'snap, crackle'," Haynes says. "I think George Shearing and Al McKibbon were the first to use that term in reference to my playing, and I can understand that. I never analyzed it, though. That was just a sound that I liked and felt comfortable with. I did a little bit of drum and bugle corps drumming in school, but I was never really a rudimental drummer, so I think my sound comes from my mind more than my hands."

IF I SHOULD LOSE YOU
from the Paramount Picture ROSE OF THE RANCHO

Words and Music by LEO ROBIN
and RALPH RAINGER

Roy Haynes

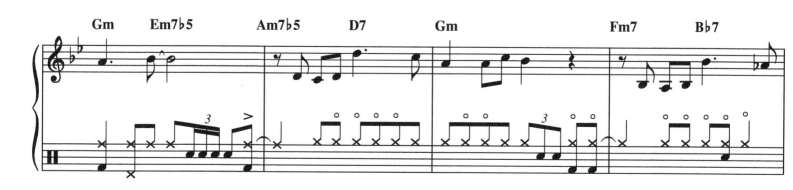

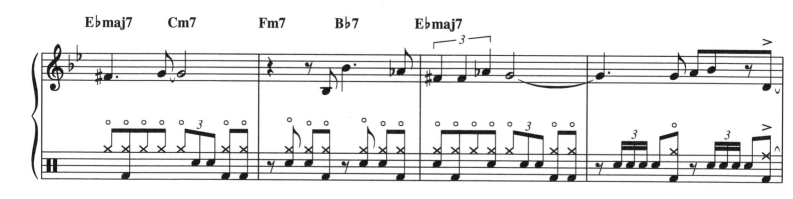

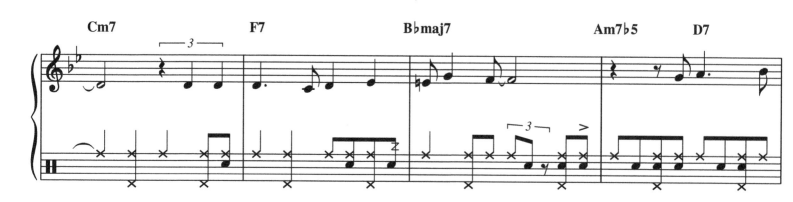

4-Bar drum breaks

Segue into solo

Drum Solo

"ISRAEL"

Album: *Explorations*
Artist: Bill Evans Trio
Drummer: Paul Motian
Label: Riverside/Original Jazz Classics

When Paul Motian joined the trio of pianist Bill Evans in 1959, he developed a personal style of interactive drumming that paved the way for the freer approach to timekeeping that soon became prevalent in the work of drummers such as Tony Williams and Jack DeJohnette. Rather than simply maintaining "time" on the ride cymbal and using the drums for accents and reinforcement, Motian used various parts of his drumkit to play musical phrases that were based on the phrasing of the tune itself.

"That started with the Bill Evans Trio, because all of a sudden the music was different," Motian told writer Chuck Braman in a 1994 *Percussive Notes* magazine interview. "It wasn't piano in front with bass and drums playing the time. It changed because of the way Bill played and the way [bassist] Scott LaFaro played. I wanted to get inside of *that*, and by doing that, then that trio became one voice. That trio started that kind of thing."

Motian's approach is immediately obvious in the transcription of the first statement of the "head" from the 1961 recording "Israel." Motian's playing does not in the least resemble traditional jazz timekeeping, not only due to its linear approach to the drumkit but also because it flows freely over barlines. It provides a pulse, nonetheless, and is rich in color.

"I never thought about playing across the barlines," Motian commented. "I was hearing what Bill and Scott were playing, and I was also following the structure of the song. If it crossed barlines, then it crossed barlines. That wasn't conscious."

In his two solo drum breaks on the tune, Motian displayed his ability to play sparsely and with open phrasing, but still project a strong pulse and flow. "I believe that 'time' is always there," Motian told Scott Fish in a *Modern Drummer* interview. "I don't mean a particular pulse, but the time itself. It's all there somehow like a huge sign that's up there and says *time*. It's there, and you can play all around it."

The ninth bar of the first drum break includes a Motian signature — a roll played between two drums. "I know I do that," Motian said, "but I never consciously say to myself, 'Okay, now I want to play a roll on two different drums. That just comes out. If I started thinking about that before I played it, I'd be behind!"

Born in Philadelphia in 1931, Motian grew up in Providence, Rhode Island, where he began studying drums at age 13. He joined the Navy and attended the Navy School of Music in Brooklyn, and when he got out of the service he stayed in New York and studied at the Manhattan School of Music. He started playing professionally in 1955, working with such artists as Art Farmer, Stan Getz, Thelonious Monk and Coleman Hawkins before joining Evans.

When he left the Evans trio in 1963 he worked with Paul Bley and then started working with Keith Jarrett in 1966, with whom he worked through the 1970s. In between gigs with Jarrett, he also worked with Arlo Guthrie, appearing with Guthrie at the Woodstock Festival in 1969. In 1977 Motian began leading his own groups, which have included a trio with saxophonist Joe Lovano and guitarist Bill Frisell, and the Electric Bebop Band with Joshua Redman. Motian also continued working with others, including Carla Bley, Charlie Haden's Liberation Music Ensemble and Lee Konitz.

Credited by many as helping define the role of the modern jazz drummer, Motian describes his approach as "playing the drums like it's not really drums; it's just an instrument that's an extension of you. The music I'm playing on the drums is a result of the music I'm hearing and the people I'm playing with."

ISRAEL

By JOHN CARISI

Paul Motian

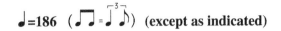

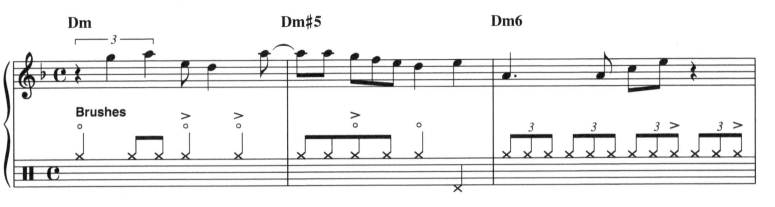

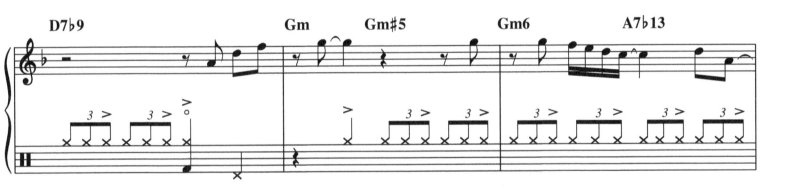

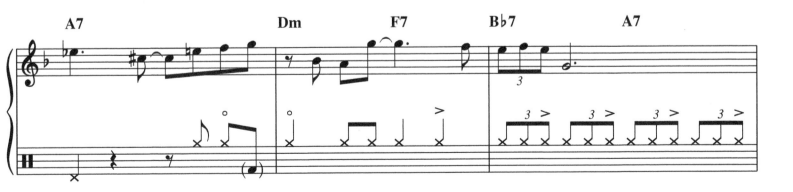

Solo drum break 1

Solo drum break 2

"It's Only a Paper Moon"
Album: *The Big Beat*
Artist: Art Blakey and the Jazz Messengers
Drummer: Art Blakey
Label: Blue Note

The unusual harmony and unique arrangement of this version of "It's Only a Paper Moon" can be attributed to the fact that Art Blakey and his band, the Jazz Messengers, first performed it spontaneously while doing a photo session. In the liner notes for the album on which it appeared, saxophonist Wayne Shorter recalled, "Art just pounded out the beat, and at the same time this tune came into [trumpeter] Lee Morgan's head. Then, we all picked it up."

During the introductory section, the emphasis on the fourth beat, instead of the upbeat, gives the tune a unique flavor right from the start. And the non-traditional chord changes give the tune a modal feel — possibly inspired by an influential album recorded that same year (1959) that has gone on to become the best-selling jazz album in history, *Kind of Blue* by Miles Davis.

Although Blakey's backing is very simple, it displays several of his primary characteristics: the strong hi-hat on beats two and four, the dramatic roll that leads into the solo section, and the drive that always pushed the music forward. There is also a bombastic quality, especially in the drum solo. Blakey's playing was more about spirit than technique.

"I wanted to become a great drummer, but just in the sense of having musicians want to play with me, not to be better than Buddy Rich or to compete with someone," Blakey told writer Chip Stern in a 1984 *Modern Drummer* interview. "If musicians have a preference and they say, 'I want to play with Bu [Blakey's nickname],' that just knocks me out. And I'll say, 'Is there anything I can do to make you sound better? What do you want me to do behind you when you play?' My head never got so big that *that* wasn't my goal — to play *with* people."

Blakey certainly did play with many of the greatest names in jazz. But he's equally well known for the people who played with *him* when he led the Jazz Messengers for over 35 years.

Born in Pittsburgh in 1919, Blakey started out as a pianist but then switched to drums. His first major drumming gig was with Mary Lou Williams in 1942, followed by a stint with Fletcher Henderson. From 1944 to '47 he played in the legendary Billy Eckstine band, which included such artists as Dexter Gordon, Dizzy Gillespie, Sarah Vaughan, Miles Davis and Fats Navarro.

When Eckstine disbanded his group, Blakey formed a big band called the Seventeen Messengers and recorded with an octet called the Jazz Messengers. Around 1949 he spent a year in Africa, and when he returned, he performed and recorded with a variety of artists including Charlie Parker, Miles Davis, Thelonious Monk, Sonny Rollins, Bud Powell and Clifford Brown.

In 1955 Blakey and Horace Silver formed a band called the Jazz Messengers. When Silver left a year later, Blakey took over leadership, and the band continued until his death in 1992. Over the years, the Jazz Messengers included such major jazz figures as Hank Mobley, Kenny Dorham, Donald Byrd, Johnny Griffin, Lee Morgan, Wayne Shorter, Bobby Timmons, Freddie Hubbard, Keith Jarrett, Chuck Mangione, Woody Shaw, JoAnne Brackeen, Wynton Marsalis and Branford Marsalis. He is one of the few drummers to have been as highly regarded for his bandleading skills and his ability to develop young talent as for his drumming.

Just as his goal with drumming was to make the people he was playing with sound good, so his goal with the Jazz Messengers was not to spotlight himself but to make the group as a whole sound first-class. "My current band is really good," he said in 1984, "but I'm going to switch up the guys pretty soon. I don't want nobody in my band too long, because when cats stay too long, they get complacent, get big heads, and then it's time to get out, buddy, because there are no stars in this band. The band is the star."

IT'S ONLY A PAPER MOON

featured in the Motion Picture PAPER MOON

**Lyric by BILLY ROSE
and E. Y. HARBURG
Music by HAROLD ARLEN**

Art Blakey

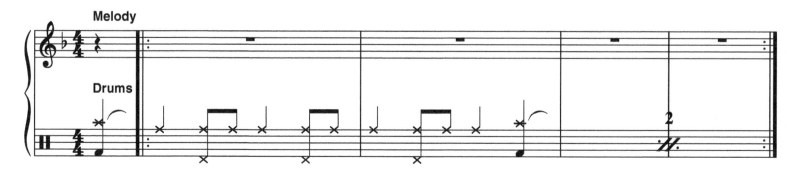

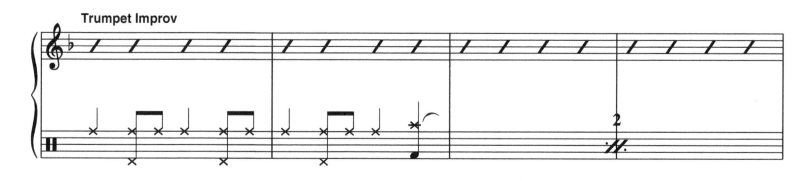

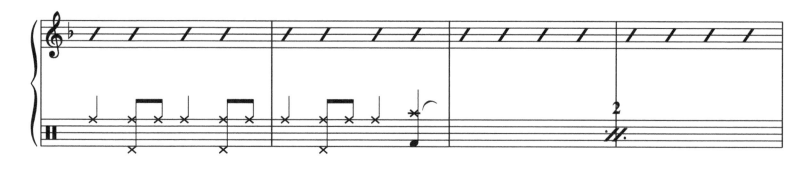

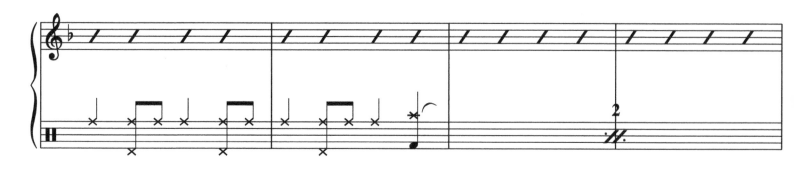

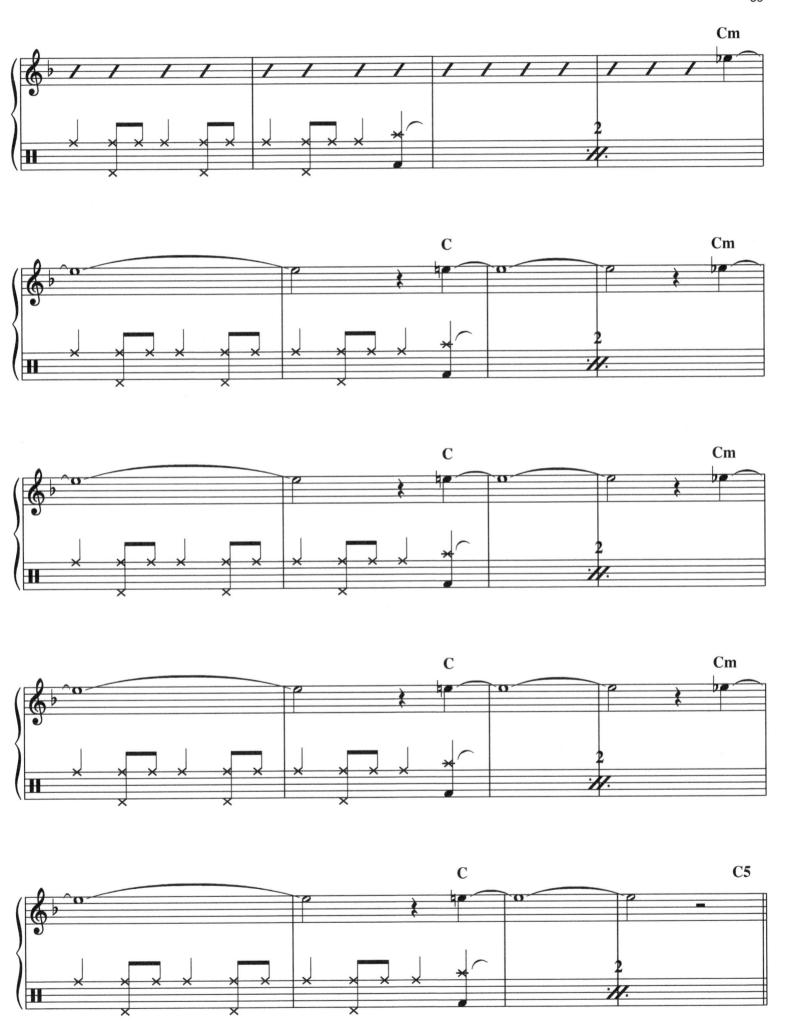

34

Drum Solo

"SEVEN STEPS TO HEAVEN"
Album: *Seven Steps to Heaven*
Artist: Miles Davis
Drummer: Tony Williams
Label: Columbia

In a life cut tragically short in February 1997 by a fatal heart attack, Tony Williams inspired countless drummers to strive for excellence and find their own voices, as he had done throughout his remarkable career.

Born in Chicago in 1945, Williams grew up in Boston and began studying with Alan Dawson at age eleven. "Mr. Dawson went out of his way to encourage me, help me and see that I had opportunities to develop my meager skills," Williams told *Percussive Notes* magazine in 1996. "On Saturday nights he would let me perform with his trio and gain valuable experience, and then return me safely home. I was twelve years old."

By the time he reached his teens, Williams was gigging with saxophonists Sam Rivers and Jackie McLean. When he was seventeen, Williams was hired by trumpeter Miles Davis. A few weeks later, Davis took Williams into the studio along with saxophonist George Coleman, pianist Herbie Hancock and bassist Ron Carter, where they recorded three tracks for the album *Seven Steps to Heaven*. (Three other tracks for the album had already been recorded with Frank Butler on drums.)

The title tune, "Seven Steps to Heaven," was the second track on the album and the first to feature Williams. It proved to be an auspicious debut. He drives the "head" of the tune with machine-gun snare drum bursts punctuated with deft fills, and his featured solo is brilliant in its simplicity, maintaining the spirit of the overall composition.

The track demonstrated not only that Williams had mastered the jazz drumming vocabulary of the masters who preceded him, but that he was ready to take jazz drumming to another level. Williams recorded several albums with Davis that are considered classics, including *Four & More, Sorcerer, Nefertiti* and *In a Silent Way* (with Wayne Shorter replacing Coleman in the group). During the six years he was with Davis, Williams developed a unique style that included freeing up the hi-hat from its traditional role of maintaining beats two and four and developing a more pulse-oriented approach to the ride cymbal, which foreshadowed the use of straight-eighth rock rhythms in jazz. Many consider Williams the first "fusion" drummer.

While still with Davis, Williams also released two solo albums, *Lifetime* and *Spring*, on which he revealed his affinity for the avant-garde style of jazz. Around that time Williams also appeared on Hancock's *Maiden Voyage* and Eric Dolphy's *Out to Lunch* albums.

After leaving Davis, Williams formed the band Lifetime with guitarist John McLaughlin and organist Larry Young, releasing the album *Emergency*. Combining the technique and finesse of jazz with the energy and volume of rock, Lifetime paved the way for such bands as McLaughlin's Mahavishnu Orchestra and Chick Corea's Return to Forever. Lifetime endured through several personnel changes, and on albums such as *Believe It* and *Million Dollar Legs* Williams became increasingly involved with rock and funk rhythms.

In the mid-1970s, Williams returned to his mainstream jazz roots with VSOP, which reunited him with Hancock, Shorter and Carter, along with trumpeter Freddie Hubbard. Soon after, Williams assembled The Great Jazz trio with Carter and pianist Hank Jones.

During the early 1980s, Williams devoted time to studying composition. The results were revealed on a series of albums on the Blue Note label beginning with *Foreign Intrigue* in 1985 and continuing with *Civilization, Angel Street, Native Heart, The Story of Neptune* and *Tokyo Live*. Williams' final album, released just weeks before his death, was titled *Wilderness* and was his most fully realized statement as a composer.

But it is his drumming that Williams will be best remembered for, and numerous drummers have named Williams as an important influence on their playing. "It seems to me that playing jazz gives a drummer more sensitivity for the drumset and much more of a rounded concept," Williams told *Modern Drummer* in 1984. "It's hard to explain that without someone feeling like I'm trying to say that I want them to play jazz. I'm not. I'm saying I want them to play the drums better. It just so happens that if you learned a lot about jazz, practiced it for two or three years and really tried to be good at it, you would become a better drummer."

SEVEN STEPS TO HEAVEN

By MILES DAVIS
and VICTOR FELDMAN

Tony Williams

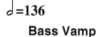

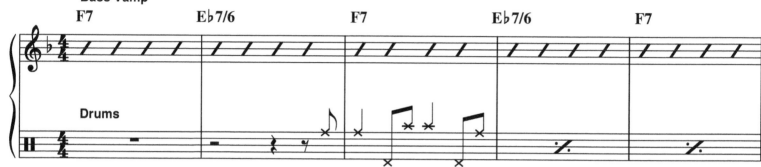

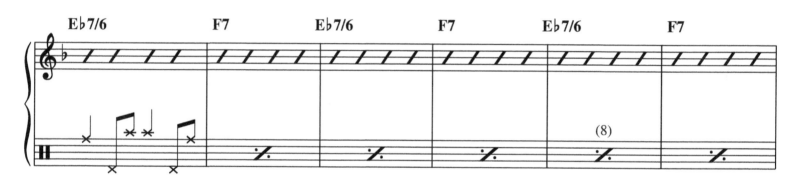

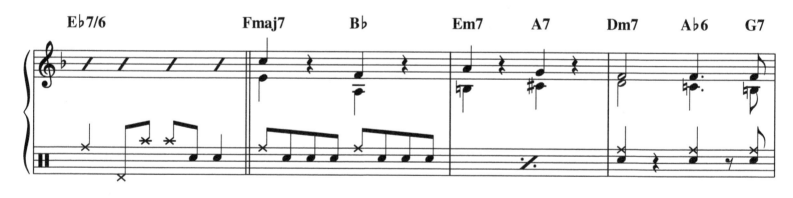

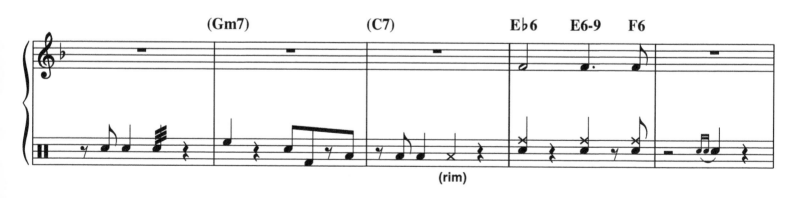

40

Drum Solo

41

Head Out

42

"SOFTLY AS IN A MORNING SUNRISE"
Album: *A Night at the Village Vanguard, Vol. II*
Artist: Sonny Rollins
Drummer: Elvin Jones
Label: Blue Note

Considered the most influential jazz drummer of the 1960s, Elvin Jones' style had its roots in the bebop drumming of Kenny Clarke, Max Roach, Roy Haynes and Art Blakey, but it is characterized by Jones' unique "rolling and tumbling" approach to polyrhythms. Whereas many early jazz drummers treated the cymbals and drums as individual voices, often using the ride cymbal and hi-hat just for timekeeping and the drums for accents and fills, Jones treated the drumset as a single instrument, propelling the time with an explosive texture that combined all of the elements of the drumkit and created multiple layers of rhythm.

"You can't isolate the different parts of the set any more than you can isolate your left leg from the rest of your body," Jones says. "Your body is one, even though you have two legs, two arms, ten fingers, and all of that. But all of those parts add up to one human being. It's the same with the instrument. People are never going to approach the drumset correctly if they don't start thinking of it as a single musical instrument."

Born in Pontiac, Michigan in 1927, Jones began his professional career playing in his hometown and Detroit, sometimes working with his older brother, trumpeter Thad Jones. He also played in Billy Mitchell's quintet, which was the house band at the Bluebird club in Detroit and backed national jazz artists who appeared there. In 1956 Jones moved to New York where he worked with J. J. Johnson, Donald Byrd, Harry "Sweets" Edison, Bud Powell, and Stan Getz.

During that time, he appeared on an album by Sonny Rollins titled *A Night at the Village Vanguard*. The fact that Jones played on the album was sheer coincidence. "I had just left...well, I didn't leave, I got *fired* from J.J. Johnson's band," Jones recalls. "I came back to New York depressed, and I was walking around Greenwich Village when I saw my friend Wilbur Ware standing in front of the Village Vanguard, where he was working with Sonny Rollins. So I just went down there to sit in; I had no idea they were recording. But it brought me out of my depression, and that's one of the positive things I'll always remember about that record."

One of the tunes they recorded was "Softly As in a Morning Sunrise," on which Jones used brushes throughout. Before the extended drum solo, Jones and Rollins traded four-bar phrases. But as can be heard on the recording (and seen in the accompanying transcription), the phrases did not always consist of exactly sixteen beats.

"When exchanging fours or eights, I was always thinking in terms of musical phrasing," Jones recalls. "I think the phrasing should never be confined to rigid patterns. If everyone is paying attention, you can simply pick up from where the other person left off, and he can come in where he wants in order to complete the continuity of the phrase.

"You can't play that way all the time; it depends on the artist. Sometimes they require a rigid pattern, and if it's required, that's what you should do. But playing with more expression was certainly appropriate with an artist like Sonny Rollins and an exceptional bassist like Wilbur Ware. In a situation like that, there are no restrictions. You can apply your technique and skill in the way you want, because that really is the way to express yourself—within the context of the composition, naturally."

In 1960, Jones began a five-year stint with the John Coltrane Quartet, which provided the ideal setting in which to express himself and fully develop his unique style. After leaving Coltrane, Jones formed his own band and often recorded with others, appearing on hundreds of albums with such jazz legends as Pharaoh Sanders, Freddie Hubbard and McCoy Tyner to modern jazz stars such as Wynton Marsalis and Joe Lovano. In 1991, Jones was inducted into the Percussive Arts Society Hall of Fame, and in 1998 he received an American Drummers Achievement Award from the Zildjian cymbal company.

SOFTLY AS IN A MORNING SUNRISE

from THE NEW MOON

Elvin Jones

Lyric by OSCAR HAMMERSTEIN II
Music by SIGMUND ROMBERG

*Left hand continuously sweeps

4-Bar drum breaks

Drum Solo

"THE SURREY WITH THE FRINGE ON TOP"
Album: *Newk's Time*
Artist: Sonny Rollins
Drummer: Philly Joe Jones
Label: Blue Note

In the early 1950s, bandleader Tony Scott hired a young drummer from Philadelphia named Joe Jones. To avoid confusion with Count Basie's famous drummer, Jo Jones, Scott would introduce his drummer by saying, "This is the Joe Jones from Philly." Eventually, the younger Jones requested that Scott refer to him as "Philly Joe," and he subsequently had his name legally changed to Philly Joe Jones.

Born in 1923, Joseph Rudolph Jones began his career in his hometown of Philadelphia. During that time, he met such prominent jazz drummers as Max Roach, Art Blakey, Sid Catlett and Kenny Clarke, who all encouraged Jones and gave him pointers. In 1947, acting on the advice of Roach and Blakey, Jones moved to New York. He became house drummer at Cafe Society where he backed such jazz artists as Fats Navarro, Dexter Gordon, Dizzy Gillespie and Charlie Parker. He then worked with Ben Webster in Washington, went on the road with a couple of rhythm & blues bands, and in 1953 joined the big band led by Tadd Dameron. Jones also worked with the Buddy Rich band during a time when Rich was fronting the band as a singer and only playing one drum solo per night.

Philly Joe joined the Miles Davis group in 1955. During the four years he worked with Davis, the group included such prominent players as John Coltrane, Red Garland and Paul Chambers, and that lineup is now regarded as the first of Davis' two great quintets. (The other "great" Miles Davis group featured Tony Williams, Wayne Shorter, Herbie Hancock and Ron Carter.)

During the time he was with Davis, Jones became an in-demand recording session drummer. "I was the most-recorded drummer in New York for about a ten- or twelve-year period," Jones said in a 1981 *Modern Drummer* interview. "I did so many cats' first album. I did Freddie Hubbard's first, Lee Morgan's first, 'Trane's second. All the young stars would ask me to play drums with them when they were coming up. Sometimes I'd be doing two or three dates a day!"

One particularly memorable date occurred on September 22, 1957, when Jones recorded with saxophonist Sonny Rollins at the studio of famed engineer Rudy Van Gelder. The resulting album was titled "Newk's Time" and also featured pianist Wynton Kelly and bassist Doug Watkins. One track, however, consisted only of Rollins and Jones: "The Surrey with the Fringe on Top."

The track was a perfect showcase for Jones' style, which was grounded in swing but had a lot of the modern bebop flavor. Although Philly Joe could be so loose as to sometimes sound sloppy, on this track he holds the tune together as a one-man rhythm section. His four-bar and two-bar exchanges with Rollins form a true musical conversation, and his extended drum solo displays his playful aggression.

After leaving Davis in 1958, Jones led his own group and continued to record with a variety of artists. He moved to London in 1967 and then to Paris in 1969, where he taught at Kenny Clarke's drum school. Philly Joe returned to Philadelphia in 1972 and alternated between leading his own groups and working for other leaders, notably pianist Bill Evans. In 1983, Jones formed a group called Dameronia, dedicated to the music of Tadd Dameron. In the months before his death in August 1985, he also worked with vibraphonist Bobby Hutcherson.

Although Jones stayed true to his mainstream jazz roots throughout his career, he had an open-minded attitude and was always willing to learn something new. "If I see a young drummer do something, I'll say, 'Man, do that again. Let me see that'," Jones said in 1981. "I learn by doing that. If you get such a big head that you think you're the greatest, then something is wrong with you. There is always somebody for you to learn from."

Note: Sonny Rollins' recording of "The Surrey with the Fringe on Top" consists of only saxophone and drums. The chord symbols in the transcription represent the standard harmony played on the tune.

THE SURREY WITH THE FRINGE ON TOP

from OKLAHOMA!

Lyrics by OSCAR HAMMERSTEIN II
Music by RICHARD RODGERS

Philly Joe Jones

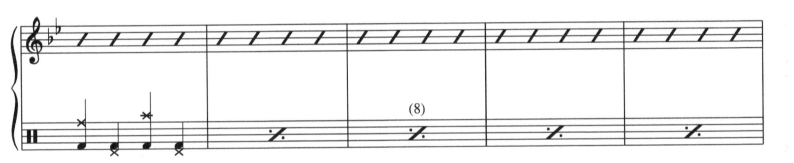

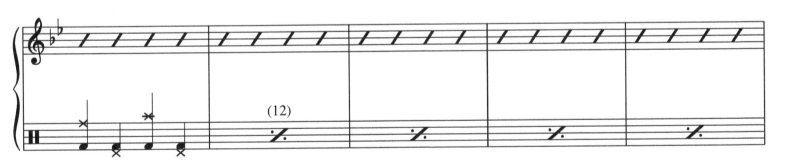

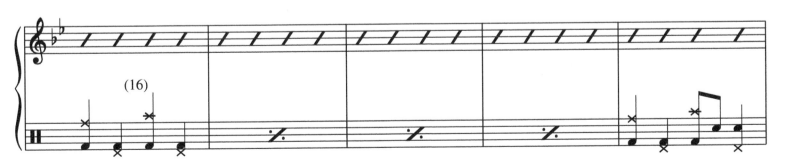

4-Bar drum breaks

2-Bar breaks

"TAKE FIVE"
Album: *Time Out*
Artist: Dave Brubeck Quartet
Drummer: Joe Morello
Label: Columbia

If he hadn't had eyesight problems at an early age, Joe Morello would have pursued a career as a classical violinist. But the string world's loss was the drum community's gain, as Morello became one of the most technically accomplished drumset players to ever wield a pair of sticks, setting a new standard for mastery of odd-time signatures through his work with the Dave Brubeck Quartet.

Born July 17, 1929 in Springfield, Massachusetts, Morello began studying violin at age six, and three years later was featured with the Boston Symphony Orchestra as soloist in the Mendelssohn Violin Concerto. By age 15 he had switched to drums, first studying with show drummer Joe Sefcik and then with the legendary George Lawrence Stone. "I'd work out of his book, *Stick Control*, and after I could play the sticking patterns I'd start throwing in accents in various places," Morello recalls. Stone was so impressed with Morello's ideas that he incorporated them into his next book, *Accents & Rebounds*, which is dedicated to Morello. Later, Morello studied with Radio City Music Hall percussionist Billy Gladstone, one of the most technically advanced drummers of all time.

"My training was basically classical snare drum technique," Morello says. "But I used it the way I wanted to. The objective of a good teacher is to bring out the creativity of the pupil. Give them a knowledge of the instrument; once they have that, they can use it the way they want to use it."

After moving to New York City, Morello worked with an impressive list of jazz musicians including Johnny Smith, Tal Farlow, Phil Woods and Stan Kenton. While working with pianist Marian McPartland at the Hickory House, Morello's technical feats attracted the attention of a legion of drummers, who would crowd around him at a back table during intermissions to watch him work out with a pair of sticks on a folded napkin. Jim Chapin tells stories about unsuspecting drummers who would try to impress Morello by showing off their fancy licks. Morello would listen intently, then say, "Is this what you're doing?" as he'd play their licks back at them twice as fast.

His 12-year stint with Brubeck made Morello a household name in the jazz world. On the quartet's recording of "Take Five" he performed one of the most famous drum solos in jazz history. With the piano and bass maintaining the tune's signature 5/4 vamp, Morello was free to experiment with different phrasings. "When people use the word 'technique,' they usually mean 'speed,'" Morello says in the book *The Drummer's Time*, commenting on the solo. "But the 'Take Five' solo had very little speed involved. It was more about space and playing over the barline. It was conspicuous by being so different."

After leaving Brubeck in 1968 Morello became an in-demand clinician, teacher and bandleader. He has written several drum books, including *Master Studies*, published by Modern Drummer Publications, and has done an instructional video for Hot Licks titled *The Natural Approach to Technique*. Morello has won countless music polls over the years, and was elected to the *Modern Drummer* magazine Hall of Fame in 1988 and to the Percussive Arts Society Hall of Fame in 1993.

Morello says that the secret to technique is relaxation. "It's a matter of natural body movement," he explains. "When your hand is relaxed, your thumb isn't squeezing against your first finger and your wrist isn't at some funny angle. The stick just rests in the hand in a very natural position. The whole thing is relaxation and letting the sticks do most of the work.

"Technique is only a means to an end," Morello stresses. "The more control you have of the instrument, the more confidence you will get and the more you will be able to express your ideas. But just for technique alone — just to see how fast you can play so you can machine-gun everybody to death — that doesn't make any sense. Technique is only good if you can use it musically."

TAKE FIVE

By Paul Desmond

Joe Morello

58

Drum Solo over Piano Vamp

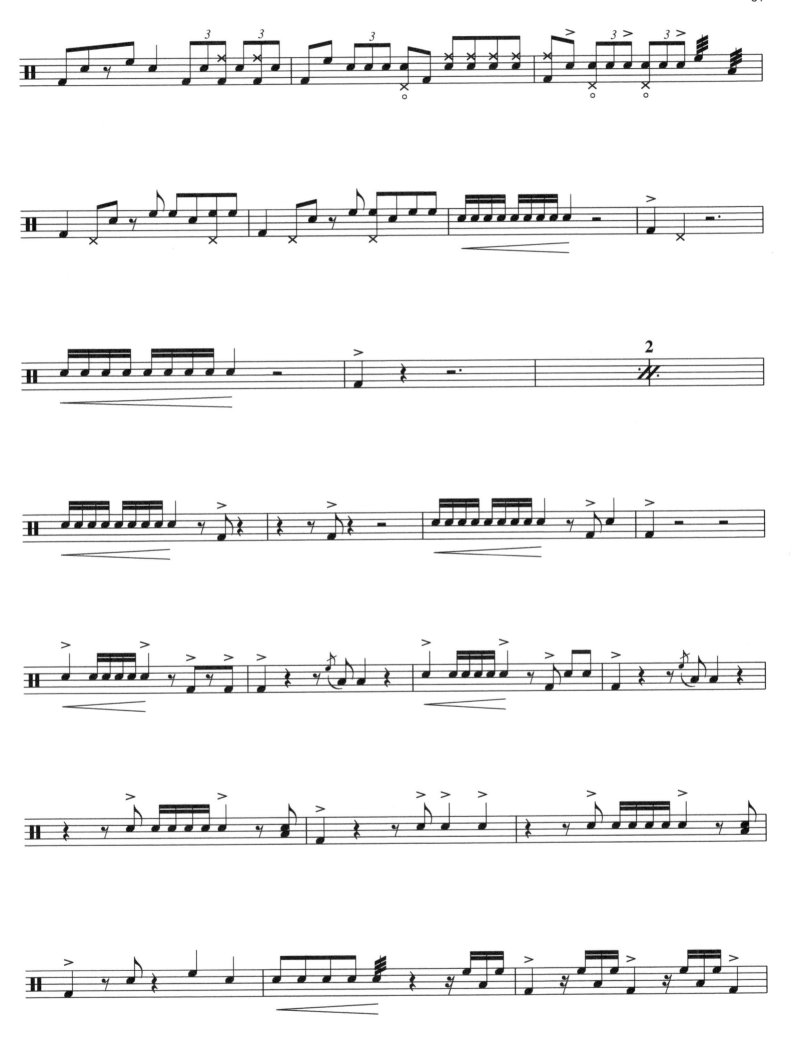

YOU CAN'T BEAT OUR DRUM BOOKS!

Learn to Play the Drumset – Book 1
by Peter Magadini
This unique method starts students out on the entire drumset and teaches them the basics in the shortest amount of time. Book 1 covers basic 4- and 5-piece set-ups, grips and sticks, reading and improvisation, coordination of hands and feet, and features a variety of contemporary and basic rhythm patterns with exercise breakdowns for each.
06620030 Book/CD Pack.. $14.99

Creative Timekeeping for the Contemporary Jazz Drummer
by Rick Mattingly
Combining a variety of jazz ride cymbal patterns with coordination and reading exercises, *Creative Timekeeping* develops true independence: the ability to play any rhythm on the ride cymbal while playing any rhythm on the snare and bass drums. It provides a variety of jazz ride cymbal patterns as well as coordination and reading exercises that can be played along with them. Five chapters: Ride Cymbal Patterns; Coordination Patterns and Reading; Combination Patterns and Reading; Applications; and Cymbal Reading.
06621764 .... $9.99

The Drumset Musician – 2nd Edition
by Rod Morgenstein and Rick Mattingly
Containing hundreds of practical, usable beats and fills, The Drumset Musician teaches you how to apply a variety of patterns and grooves to the actual performance of songs. The accompanying online audio includes demos as well as 18 play-along tracks covering a wide range of rock, blues and pop styles, with detailed instructions on how to create exciting, solid drum parts.
00268369 Book/Online Audio $19.99

Drum Aerobics
by Andy Ziker
A 52-week, one-exercise-per-day workout program for developing, improving, and maintaining drum technique. Players of all levels – beginners to advanced – will increase their speed, coordination, dexterity and accuracy. The online audio contains all 365 workout licks, plus play-along grooves in styles including rock, blues, jazz, heavy metal, reggae, funk, calypso, bossa nova, march, mambo, New Orleans 2nd Line, and lots more!
06620137 Book/Online Audio $19.99

40 Intermediate Snare Drum Solos
For Concert Performance
by Ben Hans
This book provides the advancing percussionist with interesting solo material in all musical styles. It is designed as a lesson supplement, or as performance material for recitals and solo competitions. Includes: 40 intermediate snare drum solos presented in easy-to-read notation; a music glossary; Percussive Arts Society rudiment chart; suggested sticking, dynamics and articulation markings; and much more!
06620067 .... $8.99

Joe Porcaro's Drumset Method – Groovin' with Rudiments
Patterns Applied to Rock, Jazz & Latin Drumset
by Joe Porcaro
Master teacher Joe Porcaro presents rudiments at the drumset in this sensational new edition of *Groovin' with Rudiments*. This book is chock full of exciting drum grooves, sticking patterns, fills, polyrhythmic adaptations, odd meters, and fantastic solo ideas in jazz, rock, and Latin feels. The online audio features 99 audio clip examples in many styles to round out this true collection of superb drumming material for every serious drumset performer.
06620129 Book/Online Audio $24.99

Show Drumming
The Essential Guide to Playing Drumset for Live Shows and Musicals
by Ed Shaughnessy and Clem DeRosa
Who better to teach you than "America's Premier Showdrummer" himself, Mr. Ed Shaughnessy! Features: a step-by-step walk-through of a simulated show; CD with music, comments & tips from Ed; notated examples; practical tips; advice on instruments; a special accessories section with photos; and more!
06620080 Book/CD Pack.. $16.95

Instant Guide to Drum Grooves
The Essential Reference for the Working Drummer
by Maria Martinez
Become a more versatile drumset player! From traditional Dixieland to cutting-edge hip-hop, Instant Guide to Drum Grooves is a handy source featuring 100 patterns that will prepare working drummers for the stylistic variety of modern gigs. The book includes essential beats and grooves in such styles as: jazz, shuffle, country, rock, funk, New Orleans, reggae, calypso, Brazilian and Latin.
06620056 Book/CD Pack.. $10.99

The Complete Drumset Rudiments
by Peter Magadini
Use your imagination to incorporate these rudimental etudes into new patterns that you can apply to the drumset or tom toms as you develop your hand technique with the Snare Drum Rudiments, your hand and foot technique with the Drumset Rudiments and your polyrhythmic technique with the Polyrhythm Rudiments. Adopt them all into your own creative expressions based on ideas you come up with while practicing.
06620016 Book/CD Pack.. $14.95

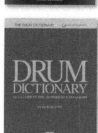

Drum Dictionary
An A-Z Guide to Tips, Techniques & Much More
by Ed Roscetti
Take your playing from ordinary to extraordinary in this all-encompassing book/audio package for drummers. You'll receive valuable tips on performing, recording, the music business, instruments and equipment, beats, fills, soloing techniques, care and maintenance, and more. Styles such as rock, jazz, hip-hop, and Latin are represented through demonstrations of authentic grooves and instruments appropriate for each genre.
00244646 Book/Online Audio $19.99

Prices, contents, and availability subject to change without notice.

HAL•LEONARD®

www.halleonard.com

0519
022